FORGOTTEN VOICES OF JEFFERSON COUNTY
VOLUME 2

FORGOTTEN VOICES OF JEFFERSON COUNTY VOLUME

2

ELLERSLIE BOOKS
West Virginia

Contents

Introduction

In 2023, I put together a collection of poems by authors who were born or who resided in Jefferson County at some point in their lives. All of the included works were in the public domain, but nearly all were out of print and, other than digitally, not readily found to read and enjoy. The small collection proved to be one of the more popular books available through my publishing company, so I decided to assemble a volume two.

While picking who to highlight, I quickly decided to not limit the new collection simply to poetry. While most of the writers I included last time wrote essays and prose, as well as poetry, there are several important writers from our county for whom poetry wasn't a chosen genre. So, I've included an essay by Dr. Martin Robinson Delany and a newspaper article written by Drusilla Dunjee Houston, in addition to poetry by John Peale Bishop, John Esten Cooke, Danske Dandridge, and Virginia Bedinger Lucas.

A quick note to readers, I have not changed anything about the work collected in this book. There are antiquated words, minor misspellings, and formatting eccentricities that may seem odd for our time. I do believe, however, my task is to simply present the work as I found it.

On a final note, for those who may enjoy the work contained

herein, I have reprinted John Peale Bishop's *Green Fruit* and Danske Dandridge's *Joy and Other Poems*. I hope to offer some work by the others in their own reprints soon.

Drusilla Dunjee Houston

Born in Harpers Ferry, Drusilla Dunjee's parents, Rev. John and Lydia Ann Dunjee welcomed her on January 20, 1876. Her father was a teacher at Storer College and minister. She was educated at home and then sent to finishing school in Minnesota, where she studied classical piano. In 1892, the family moved to Oklahoma and she taught kindergarten and elementary school for several years. After marrying her husband, Price Houston, she embarked on a long career as a school administrator at various institutions. Adding to her portfolio, she began to write for the newspaper her brother founded, the *Oklahoma Black Dispatch*. In 1915 she wrote a screenplay, *Spirit of the South: The Maddened Mob*, which was a direct response to the white nationalist film *The Birth of a Nation*. Unfortunately it was never produced, as she feared for her life if it was. Throughout much of her life, she also wrote a series of articles and books about Africa. A co-founder of the Oklahoma Red Cross and NAACP, she left her adopted home state for Arizona after being diagnosed with tuberculosis. She died there on the 8th of February, 1941.

The Tulsa Riot

DRUSILLA DUNJEE HOUSTON

This recital of Negro life in America now leads us to Tulsa. I was passing through Tulsa on the day of the riot from an educational meeting in Muskogee. Tulsa had gained the name of being a wicked, fast city and because of it many said, "I would not live there." Tulsa had a wide open Sabbath. The movies ran popularizing the use of weapons, full of crime instruction that youth otherwise never would have gained; ridicule of marriage and of the church was their popular material.

Criminals with political pull and bootlegging joins had made the city ripe for destruction. That night there seemed to be a hellish glare about the streets and amusement parks as we passed and a kind of mania seized us to get out of the city. It was but intuitional [sic] panic for the railroad station out of which we passed, was an hour later the center of a howling, murderous mob and trains were unable to stop to let off passengers.

As the trains passed through the station, passengers of all degrees and condition were compelled to lie on their stomachs in the aisles as bullets rained across the tracks where black men were holding the lines of defense in protecting their homes over in the prosperous black belt. A party from our educational meeting who came in on a later train, folk who lived in Tulsa, could not get off because of the mob and were carried on to Oklahoma City.

Across this line where Negroes and white men were battling, black people had built up a beautiful district of homes, businesses and churches of the $100,000 class, one Mt. Zion church which had just been completed, was destroyed. In this section were first class places of business and amusement, but it all went up in fire and smoke. Reports came in that an aeroplane circles the colored homes dropping bombs and setting fire to homes.

The whole trouble had risen out of misunderstanding. A colored boy had, it was charged by a white girl, jostled her in an elevator. As the story passed from mouth to mour among white folk it grew uglier and blacker. The story began to circulate that the boy would be lynched. Knowing him to have been of the inoffensive type, a group of colored men armed themselves and attempted to make their way down to the city jail to offer their services for the protection of the boy until he could be brought to trail.

The appearance of these men upon the downtown strees [sic] with firearms became grounds for the gathering of the white mob and an attack upon Negroes. As the word got out of race friction, the roads between Tulsa and other towns began to swarm with automobiles, as the cruel sought to make their way into Tulsa and to reenact the East St. Louis scenes. The daily papers made it appear that the Negro was very badly beaten. In these cases the real truth is rarely ever told.

After the riot several places contained automobiles, piled high, cars of the outsiders who had come to murder but who did not return, for Negroes had determined to defend themselves. At one park where coffins were piled high and marked in large letters "Negroes," black men investigating found that they held the bodies of whites as well as colored. Newspapers reported few white men slain but the city knew better. It was their spirit to stand up and defend their wives and children that dampened the ardor of other mobs.

The riot produced singular revealings. In one incidence a Negro editor looked out the back door of his office and saw the white man who was selling him insurance at the head of the mob which was coming to destroy his business. This leader was shot down. Among race women some lost their minds from the terror, destruction and ruin and the sweeping away of the accumulations of a lifetime.

The newspapers commented upon the mein of the Negroes as they were marched along the streets to a place of safety by the authorities--the men with heads lowered, the women marching with uplifted heads and as white papers said, in brazen spirit. Life safeguards woman in the home; thus it is difficult to break her spirit for she is the mother of the race. What man but would have been dejected over living in a civilization that offered him no protection for his home and family? It is the spirit in the Negro woman that will bear up and carry this race on.

The exhibition of courage in race defense in Tulsa helped to bring the Washington and Chicago riots to a speedy close, because the Negroes seeing the destruction in Tulsa, in those cities determined to stand in self-defense. In Washington white newspapers had been headlining a story of repeated attacks upon white women by Negroes, with no supporting evidence whatever. There was a systematic campaign on for some reason to brand Negroes as rapists.

When the Afro-Americans of Washington found they were unable to secure effective protection from the authorities, they grimly prepared to defend themselves. White terrorists soon perceived this determination. In Washington they first attacked the blacks. It was fun to ride a machine gun down through the Negro section, firing right and left, but with the fall of night Negroes stretched steel cables across the streets which hurled these riders high. The genius of the Negro soldier had come into play.

The Chicago riot rose out of the drowning of a colored boy at one of the beaches and the refusal of the police to make an arrest. Negro feeling was intensified by housing congestion and a rotten political condition. Distorted rumore [sic] inflamed both whites and blacks. White men and boys found amusement in directing mobs against Negro workers who were peacefully returning home. Trolleys were pulled from the lines and the black passengers dragged from them out into the streets and beaten.

Cars from which revolver shots were fired were driven at high speed by whites through the Negro section. Negroes retaliated by sniping and volley firing from ambush and barricade. The next day men were killed en route to work through hostile territory. White sailors and soldiers in uniform joined in the beating and killing. Sometimes you have to fight fire with fire. At last when some Negro got out and set fire to a neighborhood west of the Stockyards and a property loss of $250,000, the ardor and run went out for the white rioter. Should we let this phase of our history slip without careful recording and the checking of the lessons to be gained therefrom.

John Peale Bishop

John Peale Bishop was born in Charles Town, West Virginia in 1892. He graduated from Mercersburg Academy and then entered Princeton, where he was a student from 1913-1917. While there he and F. Scott Fitzgerald became close friends, leading to Fitzgerald summering in Charles Town. After a decade spent in France, Bishop returned to the United States with his wife and three sons. He wrote for a number of publications and, at the time of his death in 1944, was a federal employee.

Endymion in a Shack

JOHN PEALE BISHOP

I love the white body of the moon,
    And I think that she loves mine
For its strong limbs, brown and firm as sands
    Left with a watery shine.

There are no windows where I sleep,
    But a shaky, crooked stair
Climbs through the wind and the wind-swept trees,
    And the caked snow crunches there.

And there she climbs through the silent night
    And sweeps through the gusty door,
And the sudden light of her soundless feet
    Beats on the white-oak floor,

As she crosses and whispers into my ears
    Words more than wisdom wise,
And lays her slow blue lands of light
    Over my fearful eyes.

Campbell Hall

JOHN PEALE BISHOP

Night over Princeton is all drenched through
   with blue;
Over the blue slate and black massed shadows,
   blue;
And through it all, out of the thin light,
Weaving a golden web for golden flies,
The tragic spider of the skies,
The moon. Over Princeton, space and blue
   night.
It is there, it is there,
So keenly that it gives us pain!
We that are so young that it gives us pain
Feel still a cold wind moving through out hair.

You there under the eaves,
Your light
Ruffling with yellow the wet leaves,
You lover of Shelley, shut away from night,
Say, did you think
Because we did not wear

The bare white throat, the disordered hair,
The fine romantic dress,
And pale luxury of despair,
That space torments us less?
Oh! we are tired of waiting by a chink
Which never widens to light.
Now, it is a necromancer's robe of blue,
With gold worked through,
With pentagons of the color of gold and points
    of light.

February, 1917

JOHN PEALE BISHOP

Nothing moves me but mine own thoughts:
Not the fine hatred of war,
Nor the hatred which war brings forth.

But all my nights are filled with a violet-blue
    dusk of dreams,
And through the dusk
The ripple of silk over white flesh
And the wistful eyes of immortal women.

Nothing shakes my pulse but mine own dreams.

But all night long I see,
Ceaselessly falling,
Filled with light,
Distilling a rare fragrance,
Hair that is neither of silver nor gold,
Hair that is neither like silver nor gold,
But beaten of some unsearchable metal,

Softer than silver,
More lustrous than gold.

And yet, if the call should come,
I should go down with the rest,
And take my turn with the festered limbs of men,
The broken brains and the bruised eyes,
And the dead that have no more dreams.

In Such A Garden ...

JOHN PEALE BISHOP

Ah! Elspeth, that slow curve of the moon
Through the dense leaves --
How like the rounding of perfect fruit it is!
Of perfect fruit in ancient gardens
Where green and bronze and violent unfold
In this stately process of peacocks.

In such a garden ...

It seems to me that we have had no past,
No past with its old sorrows and dead joys;
And now there is to be no more gladness ...
But it may be I am foolish,
And ...

Lean your head.
So the moonlight shifts to your shoulder,
And your hair is a pale and perilous wonder.
Ah! your lips now.

In such a garden …

There should be peacocks on the open grass
And a great basin to blur
Its shadows of dark green and pallors of silver.

Leaf-Green

(A Ballad of the Blue Ridge)

JOHN PEALE BISHOP

As I went up the Blue Ridge
   I came by Barton Stone,
And the night was a night of leaves and light
   Through leafless spaces blown.

I passed into the deep forest,
   And the dark night closed me round;
The dark spray flung its mist in my eyes,
   The boughs crashed, and I found

A level space of dew and grass
   Under a quiet moon,
And in the broken shade a dwarf
   Plucking a quiet tune.

Straight from his crooked back uprose
   The chestnut's shaggy bark,

And over his wizened pallor fell
    Stray fragments of the dark.

And where no leaves withheld the moon
    A lovely lady was,
Pacing a dance whose edges swept
    The edges of the grass.

With flowers her loosened hair was bound,
    And broken laurel buds;
Her sleeves were green as the leaves are green
    That stir in the inner woods.

"And who are you, sweet lady,
    That dance alone by night,
With shivering veils of silken green
    And hair like a shadowy light?

"Your sisters died in England--
    Three hundred years are gone--
And never a ship could cleave the seas
    'Twixt darkening east and dawn.

"Oh! who are you, sweet lady,
    Green-clad, with lightsome foot,
Who touch nor crush the white mushroom
    That grows at the chestnut root?"

But still she danced, and still she danced,
    And not a sound was there,

But the pressed grass and the plucked lute
    Making a plaintive air.

And still she danced, and her curtseys were
    As boughs that feel the rain;
Danced, and the fluttering silks were leaves
    When the light has come again,

Swept low with waving arms--and left
    The leaves and the moon-swept green
And a gnarled and twisted chestnut root
    Where the crooked dwarf had been.

Dr. Martin Robinson Delany

Perhaps the most accomplished person to hail from Jefferson County, Martin Robinson Delany was born on May 6th, 1812 in Charles Town. Over his more than seven decades, he was a journalist, medical doctor, abolitionist, military officer, diplomat, essayist, novelist, and early proponent of Pan-Africanism. He was the publisher of *The Mystery*, an African American newspaper. In 1885, he died of tuberculosis in Ohio.

Reflections on the war

DR. MARTIN ROBINSON DELANY

One important fact developed during this gigantic civil war, and which could not have escaped the general and mature intelligent observer as a result of the struggle, and so contrary to concessions under the old relations of the Union, is, that no great statesmen were produced on the part of the South; although at the commencement, at the Montgomery Convention, or Provisional Congress, August, 1861, their independence was declared, and consequently must have been fully matured, not a measure was put forth of national import to sustain their cause, except the issue of the cotton bonds thrown upon the foreign market—a cheat so consistent with the Mississippi bond repudiation of Mr. Jefferson Davis, that it is not difficult to determine the source of that financial scheme, which, of itself, was an ordinary commercial measure, of every-day transaction, enlarged to meet the occasion of a "national want."

Previous to the war, it was generally conceded that by far the ablest statesmen in the service of the nation came from the South. And doubtless this may have been so, for a long period of the government, after the close of the revolutionary struggle; because, the people of the North, caring for little else than business, of personal interests, and local legislation, few men could be found among them willing to devote more than one term in Congress, or the executive departments of the government; while the policy of the South was to continue the same men as long as possible in the councils, in consequence of their domestic relations affording them ample time and leisure in their absence from home to mature their plans of ascendency.

During the revolutionary period, which may be reckoned from the Albany Continental Congress, in 1754, to the Peace Congress at Ghent, 1814, both grand political divisions, north and south of Mason and Dixon's line, show with equal brilliancy in the national forum.

After the treaty of peace with Great Britain, gradually the leading spirits passed away, either by death or withdrawal from public life, till Clay, Calhoun, Adams, and Benton appeared for many years as the only dependence of the country in questions and measures of great national import.

These master spirits continued their career till they, in turn, one by one, left the stage of action, the last terminating in 1852, by the death of Mr. Webster.

Of this galaxy, the Hons. John Quincy Adams, of the House of Representatives, and Henry Clay, of the Senate, were the leaders of international measures; Senators Daniel Webster and Thomas H. Benton, those of national import; while Senator John C. Calhoun was especially confined to that of state rights sovereignty. During the existence of these, there were other men of note and distinction, all of whom have left the stage of action. Of the great personages above named, all, excepting Senator Benton, have held the portfolio of first minister of state; and it is notorious, that although Senator Calhoun's was under President James K. Polk, 1844, a period most auspicious for the display of statesmanship, as great and vital questions of national and international polity were prominent before the country and the world,—such as the extension of territory, and the annexation of Texas,—not a measure was put forth by Mr. Calhoun to meet the exigencies of the occasion and the times. Indeed, that senator, outside of "state sovereignty" and South Carolina, as history bears witness, as a *statesman*, was a failure.

The social polity of the North being based upon labor, and that of the South on leisure, depending on slave labor for maintenance, as an almost natural consequence, the North neglected as much as possible places of honor in the nation,—the army, and navy,—conceding these, as a matter of course, in all good faith, to its brethren of the South. In good faith the concession was certainly made, because the North then as heartily approved of slavery as the South.

Foreign intervention being permanently settled, and no longer any dread of a common enemy, the South accepted the indifference of the North, and commenced preparations for her own independence. This was probably maturing shortly after the battle of New Orleans (1815), till the election of James Buchanan, 1856; or, more historically, from the treaty of Ghent, 1814, to the Ostend Congress, in 1854.

When the civil war commenced, it was alarmingly apparent that the South had by far the best officers, the North having few trustworthy, or those of military experience. And while the army was routed, and the enemy gaining strength at home and abroad, the masterly ability of statesmanship of the North not only challenged the respect and admiration of the world by the wisdom of the great executive head of the government, but intricate questions of the greatest international policy were raised, met, sustained, and established; military and financial measures created by the ministers of state, war, and the treasury, never yet equalled by any nation.

During the time immediately succeeding the revolutionary period,—from 1815 to 1851,—with the exception of representatives from Missouri, Kentucky, Maryland, and Delaware, in the persons of Hons. Thomas H. Benton, Henry Clay, Reverdy Johnson, and John M. Clayton, every great measure of national interest was represented by gentlemen of the North. So completely had the state rights question engrossed the attention of the South, that nothing could be elicited in the halls of Congress from that side of the house, of whatever import the question, but "Old Dominion" and "first families," "South Carolina and state rights," "Georgia and negro slaves," "Alabama and cotton," "Louisiana, slaves, and sugar," "Mississippi negro traders," "Arkansas and amen with abolition," "Texas and bowie knives." These appeared to be the only rejoinders given, and arguments made for many years past, in the councils of the nation, by representatives from the South.

Absorbed entirely in the one erroneous idea of state sovereignty, thinking of nothing besides this, neither fearing nor caring for anything else, then is a degeneracy in statesmanship much to be wondered at on the part of the South? Certainly not. It is but charity to the South to admit of finding a solution of their deficiencies in the statement of these grave and important truths.

Was there any one man or measure, either in or out of the whole Southern establishment, civil or military, approaching those of the North? Not one. I am fully aware that "comparisons are odious;" that these features of observations are "in bad taste," and that it will be adjudged ungenerous to make such allusions to our fallen and subjugated fellow-countrymen. I fully appreciate the extent of the objection; but when it is remembered that many of this very class of Southerners,—the old leading politicians are straining their intellects to prove the inferiority and incapacity of my race to high social and intellectual attainments,—the objector will, at least, find an explanation, if not justification, in the strictures.

I admit there are many excellent gentlemen in the South, and many have, through the press of the country, acknowledged their approval of the great principles of equality before the law, liberty and justice, and the natural inalienable rights of all men by birth; but I must be permitted to place my record, if not measure my steel, against those who tauntingly dare challenge me. It was the Hon. Daniel Webster, who, long years ago, on the floor of the United States Senate, on the very subject of disparagement, told Senator Hayne, of South Carolina, in reply to his assertion, "The gentleman from Massachusetts has found *more* than his match" in debate with Senator Benton,—"Sir, where there are *blows to be received*, there must be blows given in return."

Danske Dandridge

Born in Denmark to the American ambassador and his wife, Caroline "Danske" Dandridge lived a portion of her childhood in New York, then Shepherdstown, WV, and New York again. Returning to West Virginia after marrying, she wrote extensively, including poetry, gardening articles, and historical pieces. Her pride and joy remained her gardens at Rose Brake, her estate, which were designed and tended with the assistance of Tom and Charity Devonshire. She died in 1914, survived by only one of her three children.

Wings

DANSKE DANDRIDGE

Shall we know in the Hereafter
All the reasons that are hid?
Does the butterfly remember
What the caterpillar did?
How he waited, toiled, and suffered
To become the chrysalid

When we creep so slowly upward;
When each day new burden brings;
When we strive so hard to conquer
Vexing sublunary things--
When we wait and toil and suffer,
We are working for our wings.

Telepathy

DANSKE DANDRIDGE

Why, from the far-away
Did you send such a waif to me,
You seer with the long-reaching eyes,
You soul with the mage's vision?
Oh, on a lavish day,
My dream went out to grope,
Blind, on the hills of Hope,
And there, by a fond misprison,
The waif of your spirit found her,
Kissed her, clasped her, and bound her.
Your captive dream to be.

II

On an Indian-summer day
When Joy, before she dies,
Pants with at wild death passion,
My songs from the hills arise
To greet you in lover's fashion.

O Captor that art not free,
Bound by a dream's control
Do you miss your straying soul,
You body so far away?

Bloodroot

DANSKE DANDRIDGE

A countless multitude they stand,
A Milky Way on either hand,
Ere yet the earliest Ferns unfold
Or meadow Cowslips count their gold.

White are my dreams, but whither still
The Bloodroot on the lonely hill;
Lovely and pure my visions rise,
To fade before my yearning eyes;
But on that day I thought I trod
'Mid the embodied dreams of God.

Though frail those flowers, though brief their sway,
They sanctified one perfect day;
And, though the summer may forget,
In my rapt soul they blossom yet.

Silence

DANSKE DANDRIDGE

Come down from the aerial height,
Spirit of the summer night!
Come softly stepping from the slender Moon,
Where thou dost lie upon her gentle breast,
And bring a boon
Of silence and of solace for our rest.

Or lift us, lift our souls to that bright place
Where she doth hide her face;
Lap us in light and cooling fleece, and steep
Our hearts in stillness; drench in drowsy dreams;
Grant us the pleasant langour that beseems
And rock our sleep.

Quell thy bared lightning in the sombre west;
Quiet thy tunder-dogs that bay the Moon;
Soothe the day's fretting, like a tender nurse;
Breathe on our spirits 'till they be in tune:
Were it not best

To hush all noises in the universe,
And bless with solemn quietude, that thus
The still, small voice of God might speak to us?

John Esten Cooke

John Esten Cooke was born on the third of November in 1830 at the family's plantation, Ambler's Hill, near Winchester, Virginia. He was one of 13 children and the brother of fellow writer Philip Pendleton Cooke. Cooke's family moved to Charles Town in 1838. After briefly practicing law with his father, he began to write full time, producing 31 books and nearly 200 articles and poems in his lifetime. A Confederate soldier, he was sent to Harpers Ferry in response to John Brown's raid. After the war, he and his family settled at The Briars near Millwood, Virginia. He succumbed to typhoid fever there and died on September 27, 1886.

The Band in the Pines

John Esten Cooke

Oh, band in the pine-wood, cease!
Cease with your splendid call;
The living are brave and noble,
But the dead were bravest of all!

They throng to the martial summons,
To the loud triumphant strain;
And the dear, bright eyes of long dead friends
Come to the heart again.

They come with the ringing bugle,
And the deep drum's mellow roar,
Till the soul is faint with longing
For the hands we clasp no more.

Oh, band in the pine-wood, cease,
Or the heart will melt in tears,
For the gallant eyes and the smiling lips
And the voices of old years.

Virginia Bedinger Lucas

Virginia Bedinger Lucas was born between Harpers Ferry and Charles Town at the family home, Rion Hall in 1838. She submitted poems to various print journals under the pen name Eglantine. Unfortunately, it wasn't until a few years after her death that, in 1869, her brother Daniel Bedinger Lucas published a collection of her poetry. Interestingly, he called the collection *The Wreath of Eglantine* and wasn't terribly overt about differentiating between his poetry and that of his sister.

The Stars

VIRGINIA BEDINGER LUCAS

The Night is here--the deep, the dark, still Night,
With stars on stars, a countless multitude!
The glittering Wain its steadfast course pursues;
Proud Sirius blazes from afar; the sister
Virgins shine with soft and chasten'd light;
And sinking in the south, the Warrior waves
His sword of fire, and girts his gold belt!
Magnificent Orion! Who that e'er
Beheld thy bright meridian radiance can
Forget thy form's surpassing splendor, 'mid
The host that fills the chambers of the South,
Whose gliding steps, most eloquently mute,
Keep time to nature's laws?
                                        Yet have ye voices
O, ye stars! and tongues of flame, that, heard
Not by the ear, can pierce the secret soul,
And kindle sympathy akin to you,
Too deep for utterance! Ambition's breast
Hath been laid bare to you, whose restless thoughts
Their sleepless vigils keep by your lone lamps:
Pride lays aside her mask to you alone;

Youth's burning aspirations and its hopes,
By you are kindled; or age yields to you
Its dream, whose bright fulfillment, looked for now
No longer, was the end and goal of life's
Most cherished purposes; for few or none
Accomplish all they've planned, or even much
They might have done in life's allotted years;
But failing in their aim, yet not in vain
The high resolves, the noble impulses
That fire and renovate the source of all
Our thought; they quicken into hopes,
And feelings which remain when that which first
Awoke them fails.
                        These are the things of which
The stars bear record; nor of these alone;
Beneath their soft, congenial ray, young Love
First breathes his warm, impassioned soul;
Or fortunate or idle, vain or crowned,
The earth hath ne'er a second strain like his!

The Blue Forget-Me-Not

VIRGINIA BEDINGER LUCAS

One sweet song, with magic power,
   Thrilled my spirit ere I knew
That my native forest's bower
   Held that lovely gem, the blue
            Forget-me-not.

Still, that flower's blue-eyed blossom,
   Bending o'er the quiet stream,
Whispers to this haunted bosom,
   Brooding o'er a vanished dream--
           Forget-me-not!

Tho' our life's bright vision over,
   Henceforth we roam the world apart--
Tho' love's light be lost forever,
   In the silence of thy heart
           Forget-me-not!

On the brow of dewy even,
   When the vesper-star beams bright,

As the sunset hues of heaven
    Fade and melt into the night--
                    Forget-me-not!

Ling'ring by the lonely river,
    And the darkly-waving wood,
Listing but the wild wind's murmur,
    In thy spirit's solitude
                    Forget-me-not!

When the sound of music stealing
    From a spirit sad and lone,
Stirs a chord of deepest feeling,
    And awakes an answering tone,
                    Forget-me-not!

When the mournful muse hath spoken
    Of the lost--the early dead--
Loving hearts too lightly broken--
    Bending o'er my lowly head,
                    Forget-me-not!

Never with its hues were blended
    Youth and bloom and joyance yet,
Still till life and love be ended,
    Speaks that blossom's deep regret--
                    Forget-me-not!

A Night Scene

VIRGINIA BEDINGER LUCAS

The night is calm and clear, and many a quiet star,
    Is shining in the stilly depths of heaven serene,
While the late-rising moon peers o'er the mount afar,
    And streaks with silver light each branching evergreen.

On yonder hill the white tents stand like drifts of show;
    A hundred canon lie upon its grassy steep,
A hundred fires are blazing in the vale below;
    But not a murmur stirs the war-worn soldier's sleep.

And neither sky-lark's song, nor owlet's cry is heard
    Breaking the hushed stillness of the dream-like air;
Yet stay--there is a sound?--'twas but the ivy stirred
    That, all unconscious, twines above my window there.

Fair is the scene that meets the musing eye to-night;
    But morn may wake the battle's sleeping storm,
And when the day is done, another moon may light
    Another field of death, with furrows smoking warm!

The Ruin

VIRGINIA BEDINGER LUCAS

Where the stunted pines and scrub-oaks grow
Desert by the inmates years ago,
A lone house stands on the mountain's brow,
The haunt of the snake and the scorpion now,
And a path-way yet may be traced in the sod
Long by the footsteps of man untrod,
And still on the spot where the garden has been
Are the tall blue-flag and the daffodil seen.

Hoary and lone in the sedgy old field,
By the dank undergrowth but half concealed,
The oaken doors have gone to decay,
And the window frames have fallen away,
But a lone rose strays o'er the open sill,
And a scattering peach-tree blossoms still,
Tho' none but the passing traveler now
Gathers the fruit from the silent bough.

The stagnant waters of a sunken rill
In the moonlight glimmer, white and still;

Where the head of the fountain used to flow
Moulders the moss-grown barrel below;
Undisturbed the gnats o'er the surface swim;
The green lizard crawls round the slimy brim,
While the sour crab-grass and the choking sedge
Are spreading around from the marshy edge.

Where the cheerful hearth was ablaze long ago,
The blackberries twine, and the thistles grow,
The blue-birds build where the loose stones fall;
The crickets chirp in the grass-grown hall;
And many a time, in the days of yore,
Might be seen the bats, a countless score,
Come forth from the thatch, in the twilight gray,
Where the weather-worn shingles had blown way!

But a wild storm came, and the Northern blast
Rude-shook the ruined walls as it past,
And the old roof fell in the tempest's din,
Startling the bats from their hold within;
And now the dismal owl alone
In state sits on the chimney-stone,
Or hoots from a neighboring gum at night,
When the sky is clear, and the moon shines bright.

On the hill-side bleak, where the brambles blow,
One grave lies apart, and three in a row,
The foot-boards have rotted, and the stones at the head
Record not the names of those slumbering dead;
Should you question a neighbor how they had past,

"The family," he'll tell you, "moved out to the West?"
They have gone toward the sun, a new home to find,
And left not a trace but this Ruin behind!

www.ingramcontent.com/pod-product-compliance
Lightning Source LLC
Chambersburg PA
CBHW040202160726
48006CB00014B/1869